James Mikel Wilson
www.jamesmikelwilson.com

gatekeeper press
Columbus, Ohio

Cover Design and Art Direction
by Gatekeeper Press

This book is a work of nonfiction.

Mr. Froggy's Dilemma

Published by Gatekeeper Press
2167 Stringtown Rd, Suite 109
Columbus, OH 43123-2989
www.GatekeeperPress.com

Copyright 2018 by James Mikel Wilson

All rights reserved. Neither this book, nor any parts within it may be sold or reproduced in any form or by any electronic or mechanical means, including information storage and retrieval systems without permission in writing from the author. The only exception is by a reviewer, who may quote short excerpts in a review.

ISBN (paperback): 9781642372397

eISBN: 9781642372403

Printed in the United States of America

First Edition

READER PRAISE FOR THIS CHILDREN'S STORY

This little book started out as a love letter to the author's two grandchildren, Conrad and Arabella. The children, ages 5 and 8, live in Manhattan far from his home in Houston. As with other absentee grandparents, there is an ongoing quest for ways to be relevant, and occasionally beguiling.

Rarely do our grandchildren happen upon a frog on the streets and sidewalks of The Big Apple. This doesn't mean they are not exposed to nature. There's a lovely zoo inside Central Park, and some creatures run freely in the park. But there just isn't the exposure that a child in Houston might get playing in the back yard or wandering along a trail, stream or pond.

Upon sharing this letter with a few friends, the author was surprised and touched by their reaction and encouragement to convert it to a book. This is what some across North America had to say:

"Readers, old and young alike, will be touched by this grandfather's wish to share an encounter with nature with his beloved grandchildren. This book entertains, introduces scientific vocabulary and encourages children to step outside of their comfort zone. Lovely, tender and unique!" Lucia, Miami, FL

"What an absolutely lovely story. There are lots of life lessons as well as opportunities to widen the children's vocabulary. But most of all, the love and gentleness are so palpable!" Claire, Manhattan, NY

"This is a fun read. I especially like the educational aspect of asking questions of the children, encouraging them to do some research." Charley, San Diego, CA

"From an historical novel about Winston Churchill and Franklin Roosevelt; to a travelogue about Snickers, the family dog; to a children's tale of Mr. Froggy, Jim Wilson enthralls us with the wide range of book genres he can explore and author. He makes a good story not only informative, but also entertaining." Kim, Spring, TX

"I loved this!!! Thank you for taking the time to document this backyard adventure and for encouraging kiddos (and the rest of us) to be curious and thoughtful citizens of Earth." Alexis, Brooklyn, NY

"Yum, yum!! Nice legs!" Patrick, The Woodlands, TX (Thank goodness he didn't find Froggy first. He says they taste like chicken.)

"What a beautiful story you have written the children. You

should publish it!" Elsa, Manhattan, NY

"This is such a lovely story. I like that it's written in the form of a letter to your grandchildren but also in a voice that engages any child in the adventure of Mr. Froggy." Monte, San Francisco, CA

"I'm not going to suggest that you put this in the form of another children's book with illustrations like you did with *Paw Tracks Here and Abroad: A Dog's Tale*. I demand it! Really, it would be so enjoyable for children to read, as well as their parents." Colleen, The Woodlands, TX

"We love *Mr. Froggy's Dilemma*! We love how accessible it is to our kids who love nature and how it inspires them to observe nature---not to miss an opportunity to spot a Mr. Froggy! We also love how interactive the book is, promoting learning and early research skills." Daria, Boston, MA

"I read this amazing true story first with the eyes of a child, and second, from the Nana (reader) point of view. Both were equally fascinating and enlightening, leaving me with hunger for a sequel." Sally, St. Louis, MO

"Cute story. I plan to share with my (granddaughter) twins." Jan, Spring, TX

"Last summer, my toddler found a toad in her vegetable garden.

It was love at first sight! Our Bulldog was not as thrilled. My daughter spent many a day trying to keep "Mr. Toady" safe from our curious pup! The sheer delight that animals bring to big and little "kids" alike is evident in this story. And what a wonderful way to encourage further compassionate learning by asking questions and inspiring more delightful tales!" Emily, Toronto, Canada

ACKNOWLEDGMENTS

The author remains indebted to Mr. Lawrence Holofcener and Mrs. Julia Holofcener for the support they have given his work. And, he thanks Julia for her permission to use the image of the frog on the front cover.

Lawrence painted this humorous, whimsical creature as part of a wildlife series. While he remains better known as a famous American-British sculptor, he took up painting in his 70's and brought the same enthusiasm and creativity to the canvas.

Lawrence was the most diversely creative person the author has ever met. For a better measure of the man and his impact across a broad spectrum of the arts…Broadway musicals, stage plays, poetry, books, sculpting, and painting…the author suggests an internet search for "Broadway to Busts - Growing Bolder." Lawrence's adventurous outlook continues to inspire adults and children alike.

And, a special thank you to Kathy Wilson and Mary Kimball who, with their keen eyes and sharp and feisty pencils, edited the text and removed blemishes.

IMPORTANT TO CHILDREN

In the short, on-line interview referenced above, Lawrence shared his guiding philosophy, "Why Not?" The message, although relevant to us all, is of particular importance to youngsters exploring their interests and horizons but also experiencing fear of failure and new adventures. The young reader will discover in this book that Mr. Froggy exhibits many of the same hesitancies!

A FINAL LEGACY

After the loss of Lawrence in 2017, Julia proceeded to adapt the author's previous book, *Churchill and Roosevelt: The Big Sleepover at the White House,* to a stage play. She continued the excellent adaptation Lawrence had begun and which became his last creative endeavor. Julia honors Lawrence, and what Churchill and Roosevelt represent in today's world, by retaining Giles Cole, an excellent London playwright, to complete conversion to the stage. A premiere in England is planned for next year.

Contents

The Letter – To My Grandchildren..................................ix

Chapter One – My Curious Helper............................1

Chapter Two – The Big Surprise...............................3

Chapter Three – The Great Capture 7

Chapter Four – What Manner of Frog? 11

Chapter Five – The Predicament 15

Chapter Six – Mysteries to Learn and Share 19

About the Author – Background and Other Works ...23

Back Cover – Story Line and Mission

THE LETTER

Dear Children,

This is a true story that just happened. I would like to share the tale with you while it is fresh in my mind. Please pay attention!

Since this is a long letter, I have given you chapter titles so that you can pause the story if you need a break or get too sleepy.

Have you ever thought about why many authors use chapter titles? There are some questions I ask of you in the following story that I am not going to answer because that would spoil the adventure for you. But, I will answer this one.

Chapter titles make it easier for you to return to the story and remember how far along you are in the book. Chapter titles also give you an idea of what might happen next. But, there is another reason. They also help the writer organize the information he or she wishes to share.

Please let me know if you like the story. Do you have better ideas for chapter titles? I'd like to know your thoughts.

The excitement happened in our back yard.

Love, Poppy

CHAPTER ONE

MY CURIOUS HELPER

Missy, our West Highland Terrier, and I were getting ready to clean the swimming pool. She is always a big help, of course!

Missy watches my every move, either anticipating that the activity might involve her, or that a dog biscuit may magically appear from my pocket. So, I have to be careful that neither of us trips over the other. Since Missy doesn't like to be stepped on by mistake, she is cautious about getting in the way.

Missy thinks that the pool, all the vegetation around it, and the creatures stirring about are there exclusively for her play and exploration. We like her to think that for many reasons. The squirrels entertain her by chattering gibberish, pine-cone munching, and dashing about.

At the end of your day you are hungry and tired after all your busy activities at school and play. Just like you, Missy eats all her food and sleeps better at night when she has had plenty of chasing to do around the yard during the day. Long walks on the leash serve the same purpose.

Nana and I find it funny to watch Missy's antics…a term for her clowning around. What is particularly entertaining is that if Missy can't spot the squirrels, they come into the yard to tease her. Then, pretending to be frightened, they scurry up the nearest pine tree, shout at her in squirrel talk, and drop pine cones and small limbs on her. She skillfully dodges the tossed objects. In response, she arches her head upward toward their nest in the tree and barks "arf-arf-arf" at their taunts. Her "squirrel bark," more excited and higher in pitch, is distinctively different from her "someone is coming to the door" bark. On and on it goes, day in and day out.

Do you think you can imitate her squirrel bark? Try it. Animals do have a sense of humor, don't you think? Can you think of some other examples of animal humor and funny things they do?

CHAPTER TWO

THE BIG SURPRISE

On with our story. I was assembling the equipment (pole brush and net) to clean up the pool from heavy rain and winds that had scattered twigs and leaves the night before. Out of the corner of my eye, I noticed that Missy was very busy at one end.

Something in one spot seemed to hold her attention, distracting her even from the treats stuffed inside my jean pocket. Her ears pointed upward and so did her tail…a sure sign of an alert dog on a mission.

Take a look at this picture of Missy poking around the skimmer. She is about to get a big surprise! As she gathers evidence about some unknown creature, you can almost see her nose twitch and hear her "sniff-sniffing."

What could cause Missy to scoot her nose around the edge of the skimmer? Her eyes were focused on something inside. She even cautiously pawed at the skimmer, her toenails making a scraping sound on the hard surface. Then, anticipating a reaction, she suddenly stepped back!

As you know, our pool has two skimmers, each with a lid on top and a basket inside. One is located at each end of the pool to capture anything floating on the surface of the water. When I reached down to pull the skimmer basket out to empty it, guess what was partially buried among the gathering debris? The creature staring at me had glaring eyes, a broad forehead, and a snout peeking out!

No, not a snake. Never had one in the pool or the skimmer. Not Missy, or one of her friends. They're too big. Not a fish, they don't like chlorinated water.

Yep, I bet you guessed it. A blue green frog bigger than your hand! On the spot, we named him Mr. Froggy because we couldn't think of a better name at the time. I bet you would have come up with a funnier name like Pool Pirate, Garden Raider, Big Hopper or something sillier.

How do you think Mr. Froggy got into the skimmer? And what is your best guess as to why he couldn't escape his dilemma? The water flowing into the skimmer and the slurping downward suction from the drain inside might give you some clues.

As I reached out to catch him, Mr. Froggy startled both Missy and me by shooting back into the pool rather than jumping up on the patio deck. I was afraid Missy was going to leap into the pool after him! She started to lunge and then came to her senses.

The water this early in the year (April) remains quite cold. Plus, Missy is not a very skilled swimmer. Most Westies aren't because they are short-legged and barrel-chested. She has to paddle those short legs really fast to keep her head above water. And dragging that big chest in proportion to her legs makes her a slow and awkward swimmer.

Anyway, Mr. Froggy dove six feet to the bottom of the deep end. I was surprised how long he stayed there. It seemed like he had suction cups on the bottom of his feet clinging to the floor of the pool. Of course he didn't, and I am not sure how he stayed submerged.

Mr. Froggy thought that he was hidden from view. But, the water was a clear blue and the surface calm. Ha! Ha! He didn't realize we could see him as easily as he spotted us! Here he sits,

contentedly, magnified by my iPhone camera.

So now I want you to do a little research and find out how long a frog can stay under water. Do you know?

I am not going to tell you.

And, while you are at it, you may find it helpful to know if a frog is a member of the reptile family, fish family, amphibian family, or some other family. What do you think? I know you will find the answer.

CHAPTER THREE
THE GREAT CAPTURE

As you can see from the next picture, after a long time holding his breath, Mr. Froggy came to the surface. A trail of bubbles followed him upward. Then he started to swim around the pool, breast stroking as he kicked his hind legs. Notice how wide his flippers are. He seems to be standing on water with one front leg casually resting on the side of the pool! Could he be holding a conversation with a friend about his dilemma?

Next time you are in a pool, try swimming like a frog. I think if we could have captured and trained Mr. Froggy to swim

competitively, he might have become a champion in his frog class!

Realizing that the sides of the pool were too steep for him to hop onto dry land, I thought I should capture Mr. Froggy before he drowned. Yes, frogs can drown if they get too tired. As a side note, and just between us, I think Missy might have sniffed him out earlier in the day and unintentionally scared him into the swimming pool. What do you think?

An "aha!" idea" came to me! I decided to use a pool net to go big game hunting. Normally, I use it to scoop out leaves and pine needles floating in the pool.

I hoped I could capture Mr. Froggy in the net without hurting him. He was a very slippery and sly fellow. It took a long time to capture and swoop him out of the water. I waited until he tired himself out doing laps around the pool.

In the next picture, he is swimming under water. Mr. Froggy is a very fast, streamlined, powerful, and efficient swimmer. Maybe as good as you! I knew I couldn't catch him on the move. I might even have fallen into the pool chasing him.

Finally, Mr. Froggy needed a rest. As he sat quietly again on the bottom of the pool in the deep end, I slowly eased the net toward him. He seemed to be daydreaming, almost hypnotized. You may need to look that word up or ask an adult what hypnotized means. When you are sleepy at night or very groggy, you may seem like you are hypnotized.

Before he woke up, I had him!

There is a story told over many generations that if you put a frog in water and slowly turn up the heat, it won't jump out. Please don't try this because it is mean and is proven by modern day researchers not to be true.

However, the myth that a frog won't save himself has been used to warn people of the dangers of staying put under conditions when action might help their situation. But here is what is interesting! As I drew the net gently toward Mr. Froggy, he stayed still. He didn't thrash about or make any kind of croaking sound that might say "You got me now. I surrender!" He was speechless and motionless. Isn't that surprising? It was to me!

This is an important lesson for people. Some children are afraid to try new things, so they stay put and miss out on a lot of fresh adventures and opportunities. Can you think of good examples?

It has been many years since I have seen a frog in the back yard. A few harmless, scuffed-shoe-colored insect-eating toads, but no frogs. Scientists say both toads and frogs are vanishing due to climate change. So now you have another assignment. Try to do some research into what we mean by "climate change" and why it might cause harm to creatures like Mr. Froggy.

 One way you can begin is by asking a parent, teacher, or other adult to explain these words to you. Or, you could do an internet search on "climate change for kids." Your librarian might also help you find an age-appropriate book on the topic.

CHAPTER FOUR

WHAT MANNER OF FROG?

What kind of frog do you suppose Mr. Froggy might be? Well I wondered the same thing and did some research myself.

First I learned that because of his size, four to six inches long, Mr. Froggy is what is commonly called a bullfrog. Why the term "bull," I wondered?

I discovered that "bullfrog" refers to a large, aggressive frog. Perhaps the name even comes from the word "bully." Our Mr. Froggy certainly fit the description until he got caught in the net. He was full of energy and swam the length of the pool three or four times before capture. However, he wasn't harmful and didn't bite, so he wasn't that kind of aggressive. But, he might be aggressive around other frogs competing for territory and food.

In case you might be interested, the scientific name for Mr. Froggy's species is Lithobates Catesbeianus. Isn't that a mouthful of big words to describe such a small creature? I am not sure I could pronounce that name correctly. Can you?

And, since we are briefly discussing scientific names, I have another assignment for you. What is your scientific name? Certainly not Lithobates Catesbeianus! But, you do have one. You will find that yours is much easier for you to say even though you are gigantic in size compared to a frog.

While we are at it, when you read or hear the word "science," what do you think it means? It's a good word to know because as you get older you will do science projects in school or with your parents and friends. You might even decide to become a scientist when you grow up.

Back to our story. Something really important I discovered is that Mr. Froggy is a pretty rare, perhaps exceptionally rare, bullfrog. Why? Because he is blue! Look at this next picture with Mr. Froggy in the net.

Here is a technical answer to why he is rare. In some frogs, a genetic mutation removes some of their skin's ability to produce a yellow pigment that is common in a normal yellow, greenish looking frog. The mutation (look up this word or ask a grown up for an explanation) filters out certain wavelengths from the sun, and that results in a blue bullfrog!

CHAPTER FIVE

THE PREDICAMENT

Now that I netted him, I wondered what to do with Mr. Froggy. What do you think I should have done?

I couldn't put him back in the pool because he would drown. Your Nana certainly wouldn't want him hopping around the kitchen. Besides, we didn't know what to feed him. I am sure he doesn't like oatmeal or peanut butter. Look up what frogs like to eat.

If I sent Mr. Froggy to you to release in a Central Park pond, he might not have survived the trip on United Airlines. And, the last dilemma was what would happen if I released him again in the back yard? Probably another encounter with Missy and this same story all over again.

We needed a happy ending to this story. Do you have one?

Suddenly, I had a great idea! I called my neighbor Mr. Sumner and asked if I could release Mr. Froggy in his back yard. He doesn't have a dog that might chase Mr. Froggy around the yard. He kindly said yes.

But, do you remember what I said earlier about fear of change? Guess what Mr. Froggy did when I set the net down in the grass in Mr. Sumner's yard. Absolutely nothing! He was more comfortable in his dilemma inside the net than leaping into a new adventure. Imagine that!

For boys and girls sometimes, it takes just a little nudge from a teacher, coach or parent to get going in life or to explore new activities. Because you are a lot smarter than a frog, as you get older you will become really good at giving nudges to yourself!

So, what would you do to help Mr. Froggy begin a new and improved situation? Well, I gave him a gentle poke, and out he went! As he departed, what do you suppose he said in the the way of a thank you?

Why of course, in between hops, he said "ribbit-ribbit-ribbit." Can you say the word "ribbit?" Try it with the deepest voice you can make. Did you notice that I said "he?" Only male frogs can croak. That doesn't sound very fair to female frogs. Perhaps the Great Creator of all things large and small made a slight design error!

So, at the present, the little hopper is next door. We all hope that after he dries off, Mr. Froggy will be back to gobbling up insects.

Now that he is gone, Missy keeps searching in the net for him, wondering: "Where did the little flopper go? I just saw him here a few minutes ago!" As you can see in this last photo, she's a bit confused by it all. I think she would welcome a repeat of the adventure. But, I doubt that Mr. Froggy would.

Even though Mr. Froggy is gone, occasionally I hear him after a soft evening rainfall singing to a girlfriend. He uses his best courting voice that goes from "ribbit-ribbit" to a deep "kerrunk-kerrunk-kerrunk"…like the sound of a beating drum.

Have you ever heard any children's songs about frogs?

If you search the internet, you will be surprised how many you discover. You'll find a bunch. See how many different ones you can discover with help from an adult or older child. You will be amazed!

Some of my favorites are Sesame Street's "It's Not Easy Being Green" and "Froggie Went A Courtin'." I particularly like the camp song called "The Frogs" that Scouts still sing.

"Hear the lively song
Of the frogs in yonder pond

Crick crick crickety crick
Barrrummp!"

On the first line of the song, the Scouts crouch on the floor like a frog. At the "Barrrump," everyone jumps up in the air and claps their hands over their heads. Once everyone is familiar with the words and actions, singers split into smaller groups. Each group starts singing at different times. This is called a "round." The overall effect is of a frog pond with lots of frogs croaking in rhythm! Isn't that fun?

If you would like to hear what a "round" sounds like, ask a grown up to help you do an internet search for *Frogs In Yonder Pond-Round* by Dorothy Dino Rice.

CHAPTER SIX
MYSTERIES TO LEARN AND SHARE

At this point, I expect you are pretty tired of hearing about all this frog stuff. If I haven't worn out your curiosity, you can go to the internet and also click on **"Animal Info SeaWorld Parks & Entertainment."** Then go to "Animal Bytes" "Amphibians" "North-American-Bullfrog SeaWorld." There you can learn more about such things as:

- How to tell the difference between a boy and a girl bullfrog.
- Average length and weight.
- Diet, what they eat.
- How long they live.
- Where they live.
- How many eggs a female might lay and how quickly the eggs hatch.

I hope *Mr. Froggy's Dilemma* held your attention and kept you hopping through the story wondering what might happen next. And I hope you learned things about frogs you didn't know.

I do not recommend that you bring them home. They don't make very good pets because they like to escape and find hiding spots in the house. Then you've lost them.

What happens next is not pleasant. After escaping, they dry out like a wrinkled prune because they can't find water. Lying petrified like a rock under the sofa or someplace else, they leave a fishy odor lingering in the air. Your parents won't be happy about that.

I know this from first-hand experience when I was your age. My friend had a pet frog. To his surprise, faster than you can say "hip-hop," his amphibian slithered from his hand, leaped beyond his reach, and hid under his mother's bed. Since there was no water there, he shriveled up and died. Others might say he "croaked!" At first my friend thought it was pretty funny until his mom grounded him, and the frog received a different type of grounding!

Did you notice that I just mentioned the word amphibian again? Can you pronounce it? I won't make you look it up because you have already worked hard to get through this story. Mr. Froggy, like all other frogs, is an amphibian because he can live in water as well as land. He was born with gills like a fish. But, as he grew up, those gills developed into lungs so that he can live and breathe on land. Isn't that amazing?

If you like this story, I will watch for other similar adventures nearby to share with you in the future.

Do you know what would really be nice? Perhaps you can write me back about adventures in your neighborhood. If you do, try to assemble your story using chapter titles. They are fun to make up! And best of all, they help you organize the thoughts you wish to share while amusing your readers. I can't wait to receive a story back from you.

So, we say goodbye to *Mr. Froggy's Dilemma* and wish him good luck, especially with another dilemma called climate change. The good news is that we have begun to make progress. Otherwise, Mr. Froggy wouldn't have reappeared in our back yard. As you grow, you can continue to learn more about what you can do to help improve the climate.

Love and Happy Ribbiting to You,
Poppy

THIS IS THE END OF THIS STORY!

ABOUT THE AUTHOR

(Book signing at exhibition of Winston Churchill artwork Palm Beach, FL)

James Mikel Wilson resides in Houston, Texas. He has been happily married for over fifty years. He has a son, daughter-in-law and two wonderful grandchildren.

Jim worked for 42 years as a sales and marketing executive for

Caterpillar Inc. and related companies in North and South America as well as Europe, the Middle East and Africa. During the course of his global travels, he encountered many strange and interesting creatures. Some were human. But that, as we say, is another story.

The children in his life, both in his own family and families of friends and neighbors, inspired this true story about Mr. Froggy. It started out as a love letter with no intention of becoming a book.

Jim's sense of geography, nature, and history is incorporated into this book as well as two others. They are titled *Churchill and Roosevelt: The Big Sleepover at the White House* and *Paw Tracks Here and Abroad: A Dog's Tale*.

Hopefully, when they are older, children will be inspired by Winston Churchill and Franklin Roosevelt's compassion, faith, resiliency, and sense of the greater good as told in *Churchill and Roosevelt: The Big Sleep Over at the White House.* This book is about the three weeks that Prime Minister Winston Churchill lived in the White House with the Roosevelts from Christmas 1941 – New Year 1942.

The bond that was created between Franklin Roosevelt and Winston Churchill and the decisions made during that period arguably determined the course of WWII. The aftermath of their decisions affects the world today.

Paw Tracks Here and Abroad: A Dog's Tale, written for "children of all ages," takes us on the true adventures of a stray dog who travels half way around the world, escapes four times, and possesses a strong will to survive. It teaches some geography, a little history, and the importance of good veterinarian care, nutrition, grooming, playtime and thoughtful kennel boarding.

Snickers, the principal character, shares in first person (or first dog) her marvelous and weird adventures over a 22-year life span. The book itself was begun in 2000 by the author, and it took another 12 years for Snickers to fully find her voice.

Proceeds from *Paw Tracks Here and Abroad: A Dog's Tale* are donated to the American Society for the Prevention of Cruelty to Animals (ASPCA) in support of their many missions on behalf of animals. Proceeds from *Churchill and Roosevelt: The Big Sleepover at the White House* are divided evenly between the National Churchill Museum, Fulton, Missouri and The Fallen Warriors Memorial, Houston, Texas. Both books have earned numerous 5 Star Amazon book postings from readers.

Jim is a member of The Authors Guild. More about the above books and entertaining free blogs are available on his website: www.jamesmikelwilson.com.

www.ingramcontent.com/pod-product-compliance
Ingram Content Group UK Ltd.
Pitfield, Milton Keynes, MK11 3LW, UK
UKHW060216240426
12048UKWH00030BB/1687

9 781642 372397